The Flowers Never Really Grew

The Flowers Never Really Grew

ISBN 978-0-6456224-0-9

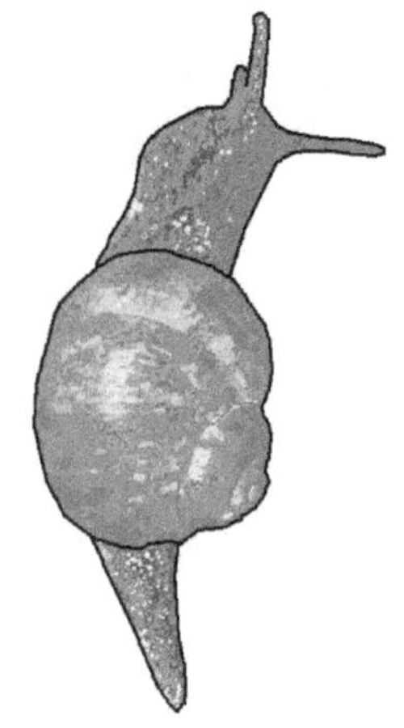

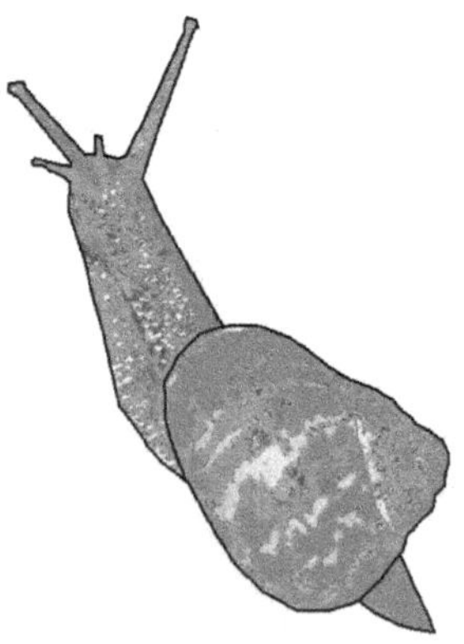

The Flowers Never Really Grew

A Murderer in the Mirror

She was sitting in the corner
of a room so dark and quiet
The light had all been drained
from what used to be a riot

A place so dark she could not see
the sharply pointed blade
in the hand of her killer when she
was dismissed and set to fade

Nobody noticed her gone
They didn't lose concentration
It wasn't the talk of the town
Not a single mind was shaken

The killer knew her well
He knew that she would go
Nobody would miss her
They did not like her so

Upon this dreary evening,
that no one seemed to mourn,
a sad girl lost her misery
No longer to be forlorn

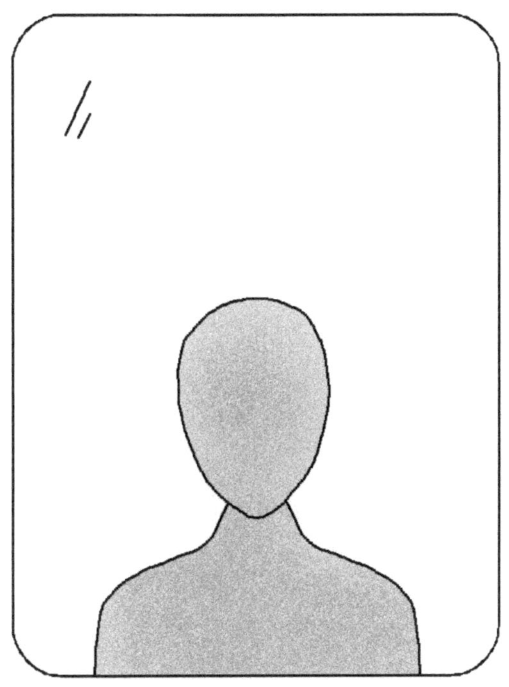

Dear Heart

Time to die oh pretty heart
Your light is gone now fall apart
If only I would miss you so
But that won't happen. Now you know

So fade away you wretched heart
How long is left until we must part?
I cannot say I won't forget
how you were once my safety net

Leave me now, be gone my heart
Oh how I wish you would depart
War won't end till the battle's won
It's all gone now so you are done

Your time is up poor withered heart
You were there right from the start
Those times you caught me when I fell
Now I've let go so say farewell

Sleep

Little sounds escaping the silence
Emptiness flooding through
Surrounding us in hatred
Alone and confused

Nausea taking over
Invisible in our minds
Colliding with the past
Do we even have a future?

Lay down your head, sweet angel
Empty your mind
and finally
sleep.

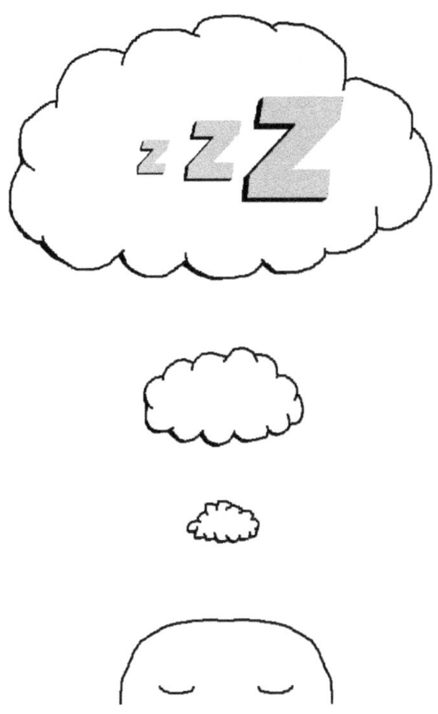

z z Z

Late Night Pondering

Even stars will crumble
Shattering apart
Silently they cry
as light fades into dark

Happiness can be rebuilt
Turn it all around
Smiles can be flipped over
and turned into a frown

But can it go the other way?
I wonder to myself
Can we fix what has been broken
or do we all just need some help?

Rainbows soon will fade away
and skies will turn to black
For all these things to stay the same
is the one thing that they lack

What is change when we put it in words
but a war inside our heads?
Sometimes for better, others for worse
Though all constant till the end

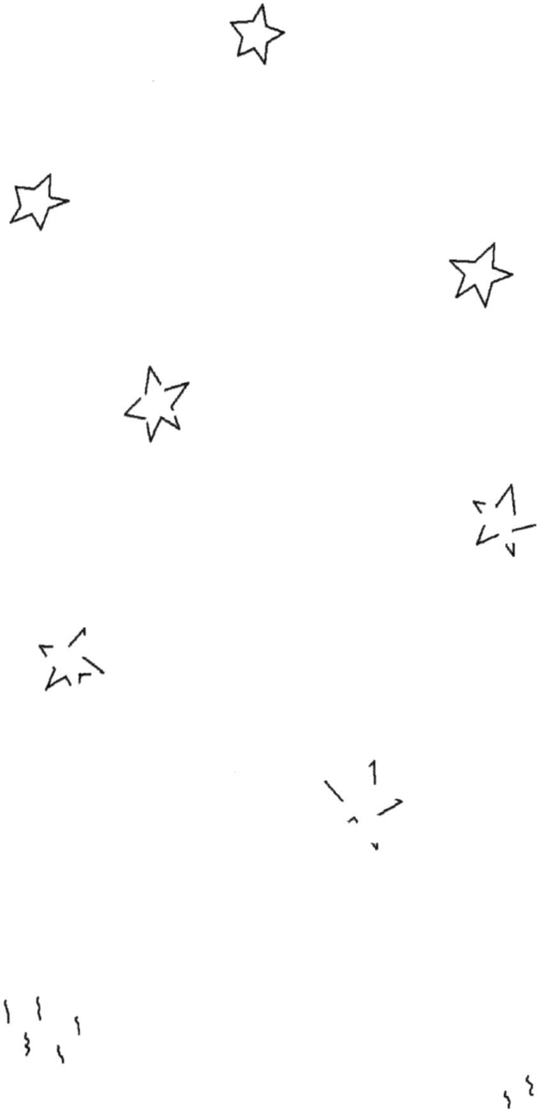

The Captain

My soul is a sinking ship
I'm falling beneath the waves
My mind acts as an anchor
sinking deeper every day

My heart is like a tidal wave
Smothering me alive
It's harder breathing every day
It's getting harder to try

You were the sails that kept me floating
stopped me from falling through
but our trust has become broken
and there's nothing I can do

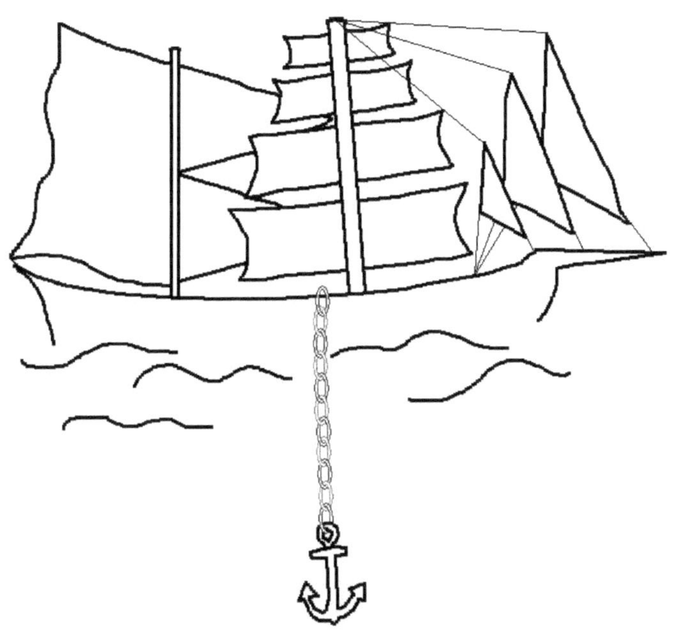

Falling Again

Little children, falling fast
Growing up, run from the past
Fade together, black me out
We are never getting out

No escape from tired eyes
Same old faces, same old lies
Moving slower, we're still here
Another moment, another year

We have our poisons and a knife
Destroyers of our very own life
We hurt ourselves to end the pain
But only to end up falling again

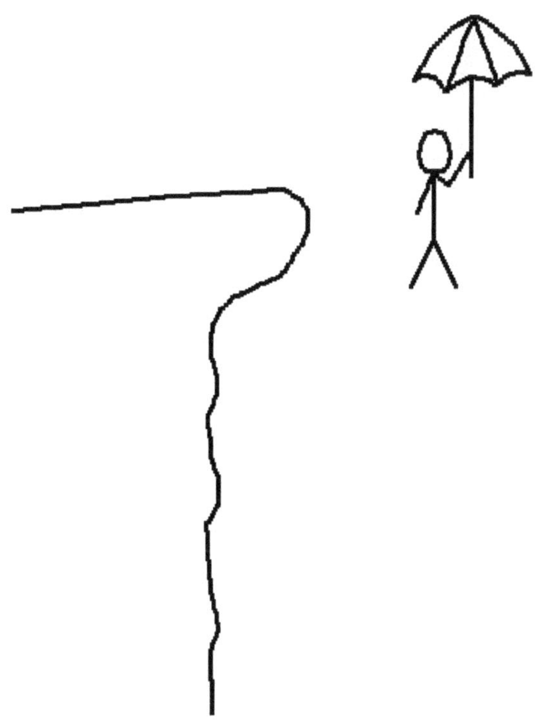

You, So Quiet

You, so quiet
Your mind so deep in thought
Your eyes, absent
as if sight was never taught

Gazing far
Is there something I cannot see?
Awkward silences
as if they define me

Inevitable
The way I break so much
A dangerous poison
always coming with your touch

Apologies
Repeated often from fear
The constant "I'm sorry"
becomes annoying to hear

Thoughts and ideas
that I can't ever speak
Wishes and dreams
that never reach their peak

You, so quiet
Your mind so deep in thought
Your eyes, absent
as if sight was never taught

And I, so lost
I ponder on my own
A feeling, strange
It seems so far from home

Calm when I can be
Safety's less than a lie
It can't be, I've known it
But can it stay alive?

Your arms, as you held me
I lost all of my fears
The warmth took all that
I'd hidden for years

Memories in me
Hidden, not out of sight
Allow them to fade
Allowing me to fight

You, so quiet
Your mind so deep in thought
Your eyes, absent
as if sight was never taught

A hug. Small.
A simple embrace.
Words unspoken
held in their place

A thought, unsafe
I'll keep it hidden from you
Dangerous ideas
They'll stay out of your view

Secrets unspoken
are what keeps us safe
Share them, it's broken
Our lives get in the way

A secret I told
to a saviour, a friend
Remaining unbroken
or to soon reach an end

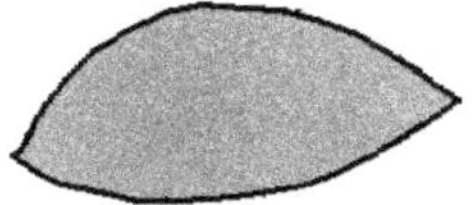

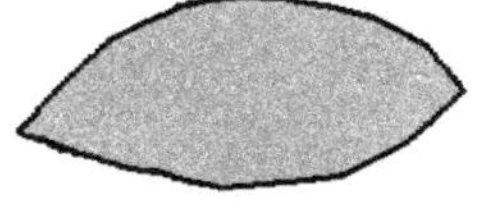

The Panic State

You've got a labyrinth inside of your mind
All these cold thoughts left in twisted rhymes
You're shaking, it's something that you can't control
Questions unanswered are taking their toll

Don't give up hope on all these long lost dreams
They'll push until your sanity is splitting at the seams
You're freezing, hold on, now it's getting too hot
Back inside your mind again, I think we're getting lost

Drag me down, but don't pull me to your level
when everything you do keeps on leaving me dishevelled
You're crying, through your eyes come these fountains of tears
Remembering the memories you've hidden all these years

They'll bring us down just to leave us when we're broken
Reminding us to leave whatever thoughts we have unspoken
You're struggling to breathe now, is this what they wanted?
To wedge themselves into our minds and leave us to be haunted?

I've had these kind of thoughts ever since I was a child
They like to believe we're not broken, that we're wild
You're holding back, trying hard not to throw up
They're always telling you they wish that you'd just grow up

Do you see what they're doing to our innocent lives?
Can you see the hurt they bring to us, more deadly than knives?
You're frozen, you don't know what else you can do
Keep pushing on the barriers until you make it through

Their words crush us faster than it takes for them to speak
Cruel and heartless taunts that can make us feel so bleak
You're fighting, your heart's beating faster than it should
Forget about the negatives, just think about what's good

They'll try to crush you, please just keep standing tall
I know you'll rise back stronger every time they make you fall
You're doing well, you know that soon you'll be fine
I know it's hard to win, just give it some time

Broken bones will mend, but a mind cannot heal
Nothing can replace what you can't physically feel
You're okay now, there's not much left you can do
Just remember when you break that you'll always make it through

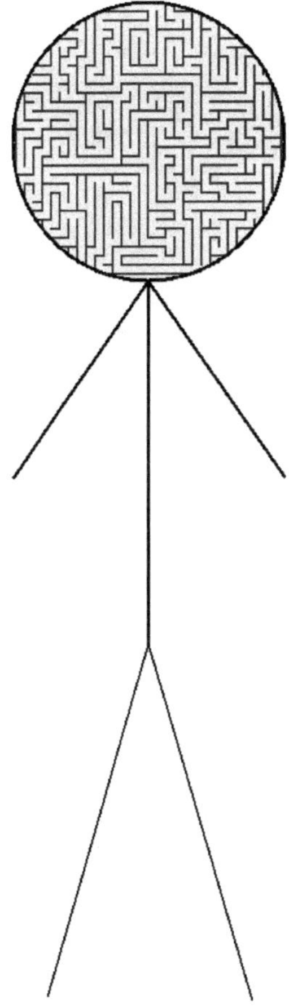

I Am a Person, I Exist

I am a person. I exist.
Not a man, nor a woman
Nothing special, my skin just fits

I am a person. I exist.
I don't want your labels
or your judgmental bullshit

I am a person. I exist.
I don't need your approval
I'm a human being. That is it.

I am a person. I exist.
Calling out society
I'll say "I'm sick of this"

I am a person. I exist.
Screw your gender roles
Life's not all about your bits

I am a person. I exist.
Where's the equality?
Because THIS isn't it.

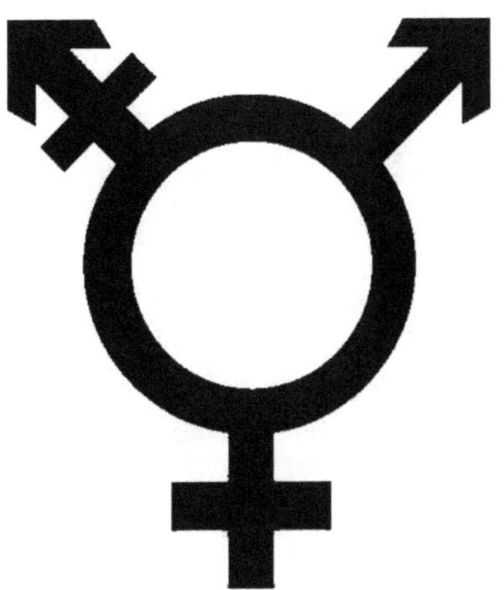

Hope Wears a Facade

Brown eyes that hide a disguise
As warm as the sun in the sky
Warm heart, don't tear it apart
Darling, your world is too kind

Soft skin something's boiling within
Tell me it's not worth a try
Broken dreams all torn at the seams
Remember your thoughts late at night

Safe arms to keep us from harm
They'll tell us our lives are all wrong
Daft little fears we'll hold close for years
Never knowing where we can belong

Search for a place where we can feel safe
What we should've had all along
A feeling like choking, now I'm just hoping
we can find the will to stay strong

So many days, here's a reason to stay
Remember the past isn't now
You're feeling done, still better than some
We've made it this far, not sure how

Smiling face, get me out of this place
Don't you ever put on a frown
No time to play, please don't go away
Don't leave me alone while I drown

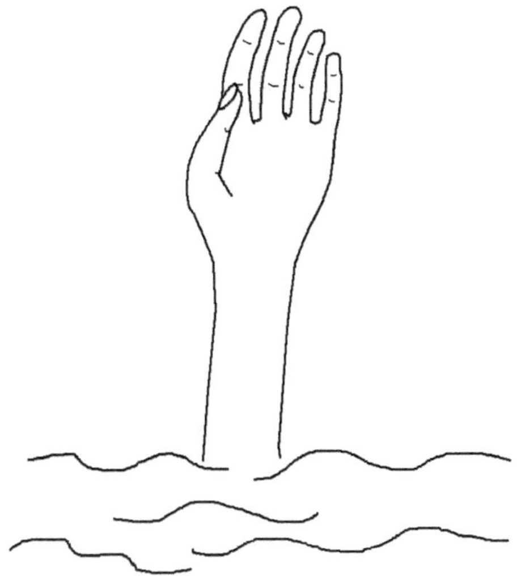

Faded Hearts

Like pieces of a puzzle you can't break us apart
Home is where the heart is but it's you that holds my heart
Why is it now, so suddenly, we're tearing at the edge?
What we had began so dear, but now promises turn to dread

Our picture's slowly fading, I see it in your eyes
Like we ground it on the pavement looking for some kind of
prize
Love is not a game, no, it cannot be won
Fear is not to blame, we're just coming undone

What once appeared perfection now feels like another chore
It's hard to point the moment when we lost what we came for
Still time goes by and comes as fast, just like it did before
Now faded hearts and memories replace the love we share no
more

Sometimes

Do I drink because I miss you,
or do I miss you because I drink?
Sometimes the words 'I miss you' are
all I can seem to think

Do we break because we're broken,
or are we broken because we break?
Sometimes we think important things
aren't more than a mistake

Do we hurt because we're empty,
or are we empty because we hurt?
Sometimes the only way to rise
is to first fall in the dirt

Do we dream because we're hopeless,
or are we hopeless because we dream?
Sometimes the things we hope for
aren't just what they seem

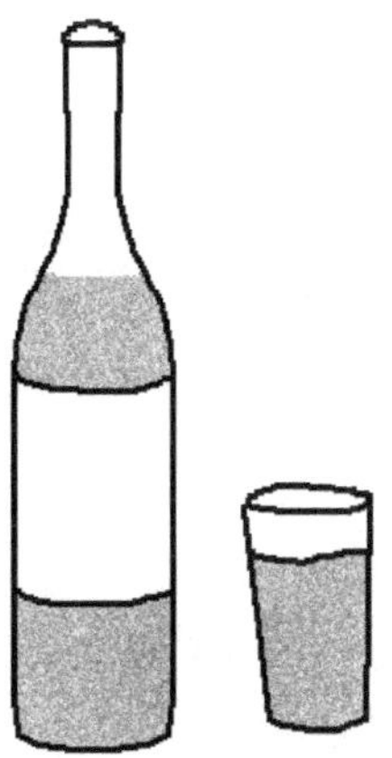

He Waits

I shouldn't have to say I'm sorry
for things I did that were not wrong
But now here I sit and worry
that you think you don't belong

Those hidden things you cannot see
Take a deep breath, and let it go
Confess your awful thoughts to me
We can take this nice and slow

Take your heart, unravel it
Your journey's just begun
So many parts that seem to fit
You'll have to choose just one

You shouldn't say what you don't mean
Don't hide the truth in lies
I'll see the words left in between
The secrets you disguise

Was your goal for me to fall?
To make me run away?
I said I'd be here through it all
I promised you I'd stay

Take your dreams, spread them around
Do whatever it takes to forget
Pay close attention to the sounds
Each word is an empty threat

She shouldn't have to ignore the truth
Ignore what she knows is real
The tales we hear of broken youth
that didn't take the time to heal

The dreams we had, the times we shared
I never thought we'd fade
Some people like to feign they cared
Forget the memories we made

Take your ideas, set them free
Embrace me, hold me tight
The nagging thoughts, just let them be
Just do whatever's right

He shouldn't have to tell you
everything that's on his mind
Calm down, you'll make it through
Move forward, don't rewind

Perhaps one day you'll find the truth
Maybe then you'll know
things aren't lies without the proof
Just a portion of the show

Take your wishes, make them real
Do what you feel you should
The power to give and the power to steal
Use them both for good

They shouldn't have to pretend
that everything's okay
We're all just waiting for the end
in our own different ways

Forgetting all the lives we've lost
to people having fun
Why should a life be the cost?
What's this horror we've begun?

Take your nightmares, let them out
Stay calm and don't be scared
You sit and whisper while I shout
I hope you came prepared.

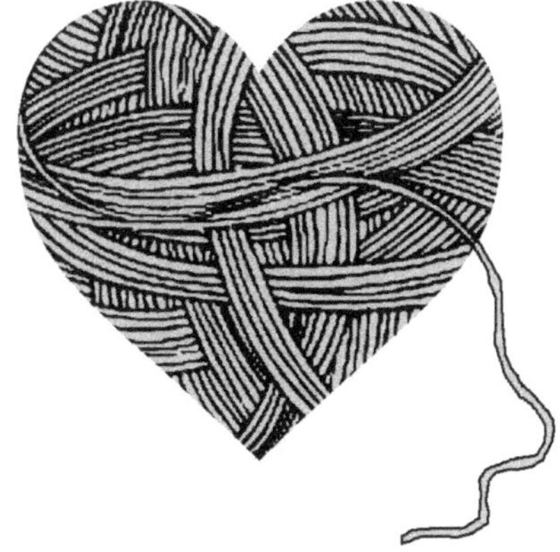

Blossom

Plant another flower
and watch it try to bloom
as you leave it all alone
in a cold, dark room

You expect something to blossom
without letting in the light
You're begging it to go
but it won't without a fight

Throw it on the floor
Watch the leaves all start to bruise
Question what else there is
for a flower left to lose

Fill the pot with poison
Watch the flower lose some colour
But still it keeps on standing
as you still try to make it duller

The flower soon will dry out
You watched and helped it fall apart
Beauty never had a chance
It was broken from the start

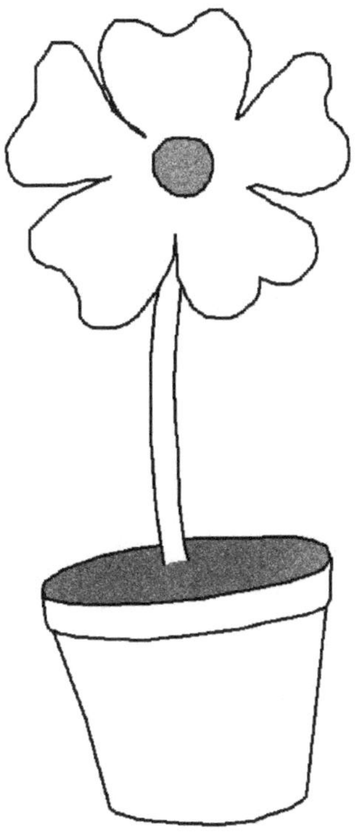

Doors of Life

Open
The first breath
Fingernails like grains of rice

Closed
The punishment
For silly spoken lies

Open
A friendship
And learning how to play

Closed
We lose them
When childhood slips away

Open
New ideas
And knowledge that excludes them

Closed
The critics
We learn to listen to them

Open
Our dreams
And goals we wish to meet

Closed
Denials
Small whispers of defeat

Open
A family
The people made to care

Closed
We grow up
They were never really there

Open
Employment
We work so we can live

Closed
Retire
They took all we could give

Open
Freedom
That small time that remains

Closed
The end
Our lives lost in our age

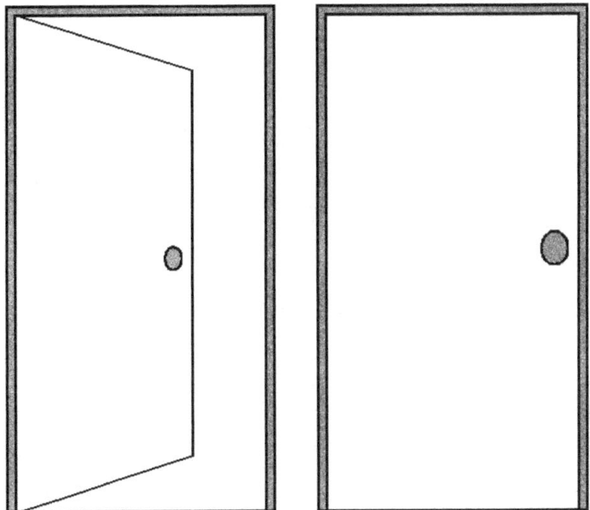

Break

Break me down
Break apart my body, tear the pieces off one by one...
by one.
Spill whatever fluids may rest within me
For faith
For decade-old beliefs
For misunderstanding and the unwillingness to learn
For . . . nothing.
Break me down
Watch me as I tremble
Sit blindly as I fall to the ground before you and throw what-
ever hope I had out the proverbial window
Watch me as I turn to ash
To dust
To the final whisper in the wind
To . . . nothing.
Break me down
Tear the beating heart out of the chest-cage that holds it so
well
So tightly it could break at times, but it keeps
on
beating.
And sometimes it just hurts.
Sometimes it hurts, not just in one sense, but as both inter-
nal and external forms of pain
Both the feelings I think and feel as a being with the capa-
bilities of holding emotion and as the physical strength of a
rhinoceros sitting sturdily upon my chest
Until I am
nothing.

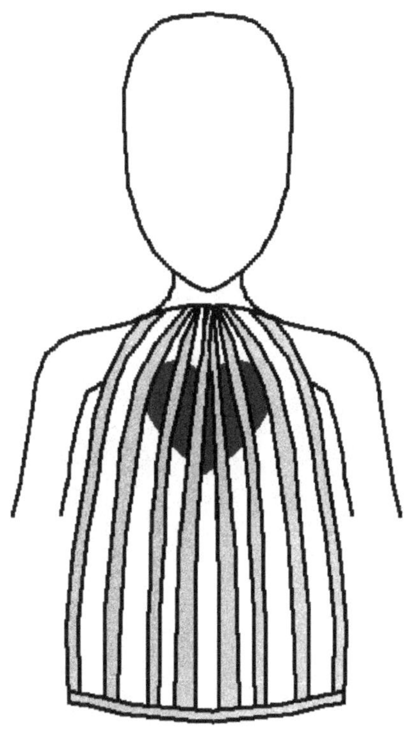

Drowning

The air feels like water
and I'm drowning in it
No edge of the lake
and no way to breathe

When I tried to swim away
I found myself sinking deeper
and now the darkness is overwhelming
What happened to the light?

The light stayed above the water
and I don't know how to swim
No. I can't swim.
I'm still sinking

I never had a life jacket
No boat to pull myself up onto
Only an anchor wrapped around my feet
pulling
me
down

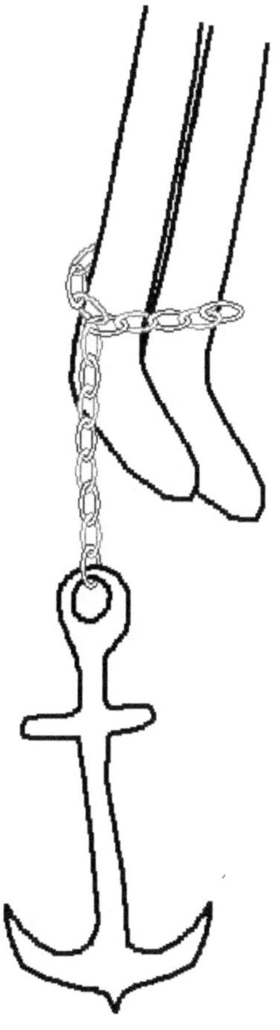

Enough

I'm not enough of a boy?
You forced me into this dress
Spouting your lies and bullshit
just to put me in distress

I'm not enough of a person
to be welcome in your eyes
Trying to make me hate you
Wishing I'd live in disguise

Not enough of what you wanted
Too honest and too me
Enough to leave you haunted
with all that I could have been

Not enough to fit the image
that you'd conjured in your mind
You'll soon find that you've wasted
all the dreams you'd wished to find

I'm enough of who I want to be
to make my world my own
and not need to surrender
to fall down and call it home

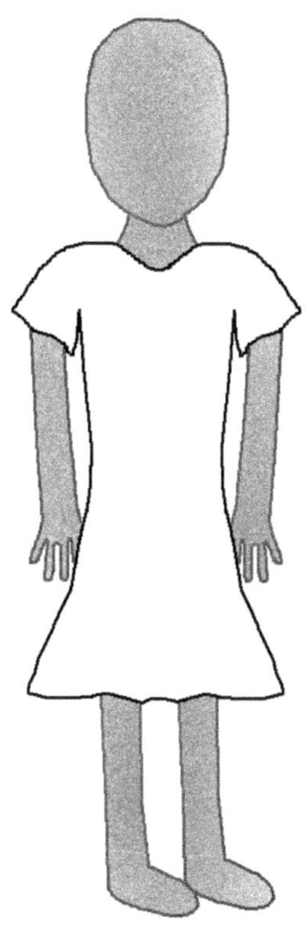

Lola

Listen to me
Lock me up in your mind
I'll save you from the fears
you just can't leave behind

Only a dream, but
I'm here when you're awake
I'll keep you grounded
when the risks seem hard to take

Love and absence
are constantly at war
Holding you back from
the things you're fighting for

Always remember
you're never truly lost
and sometimes dreams may
be worth more than they cost

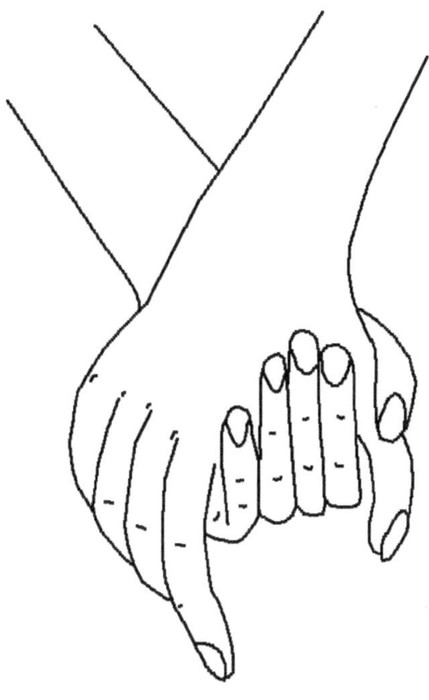

Endings

Opposing the light
I turn toward the abyss
The undying darkness comforts me
Swallowed whole and consumed
by a sea of mystery

Reflections play tricks
though I'm not easy to fool
The miscommunication wears thin
Endings seem so simple
The hard part is to begin

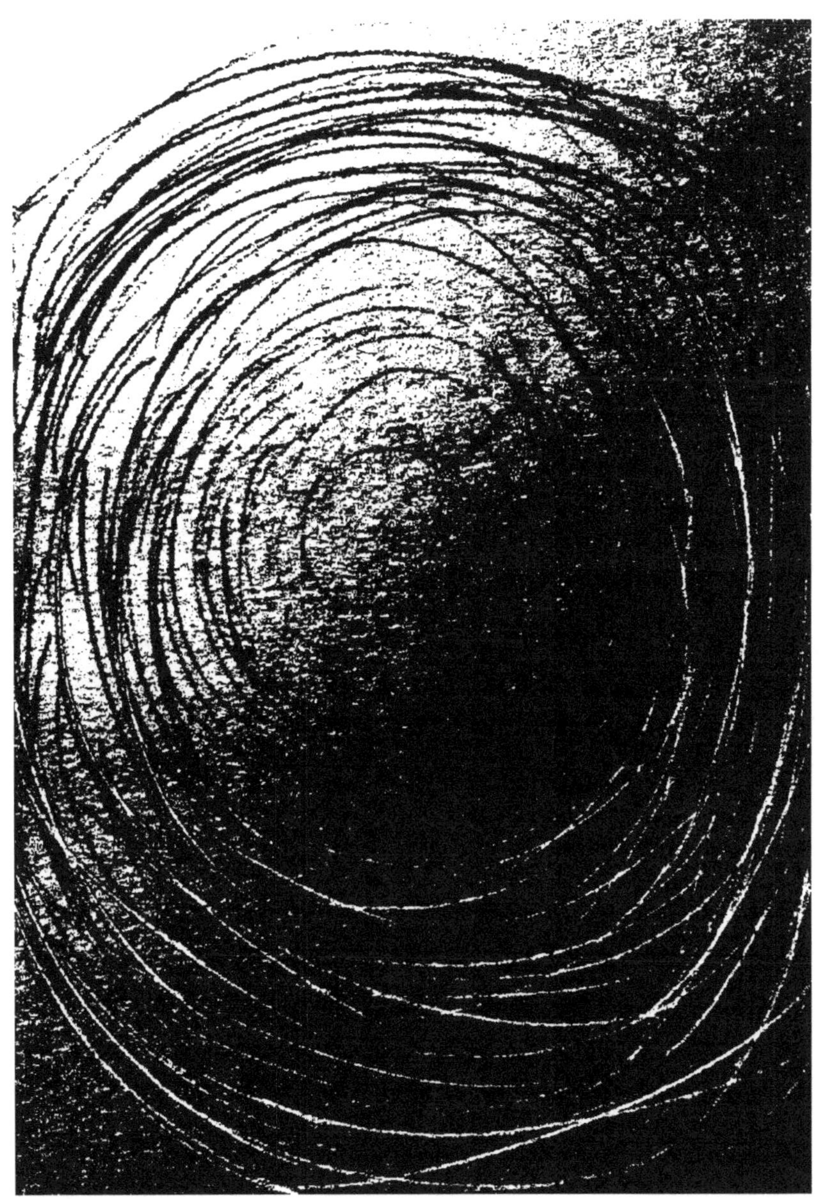

Suffocate

How long until the sky falls
and crushes all my dreams?
How many times have things been
so far from what they seem?
When understanding moulds intent
we all know what we mean

How long before the ocean comes
to swallow all my fears?
How many days do people spend
drying their chins from tears?
When consciousness evades the living
silence is all I hear

How long until the earth reaches
to pull me underground?
How many years do people stay
waiting to be found?
When expectation lifts us up
the future won't be bound

How long until the air surrounds
my lungs and chokes them dry?
How many wrong falls must we take
until we learn to fly?
When any choice is locked away
so is the chance to try
to find a peaceful way to live
until we fade or die

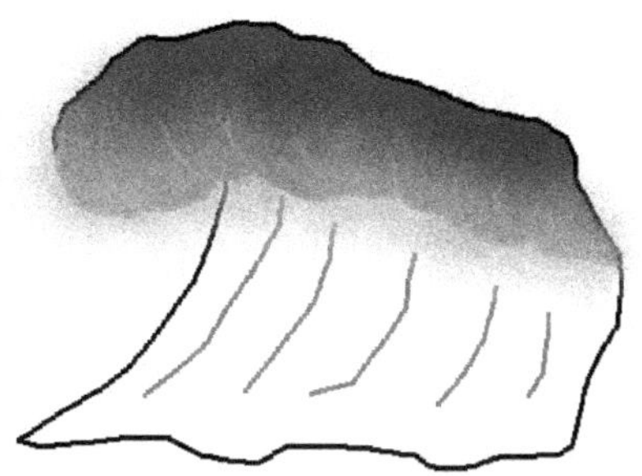

Caged

Trapped
in a world that screams
Yells
in an indefinite silence
Howling
like wind in a storm
Frozen
Unable to get warm
Lost
in a maze that won't end
Stop
You don't need to pretend
Live
until you can no more
Gone
Stepping through the door
Silence
as it grips your throat
Darkness
slipping as you
choke

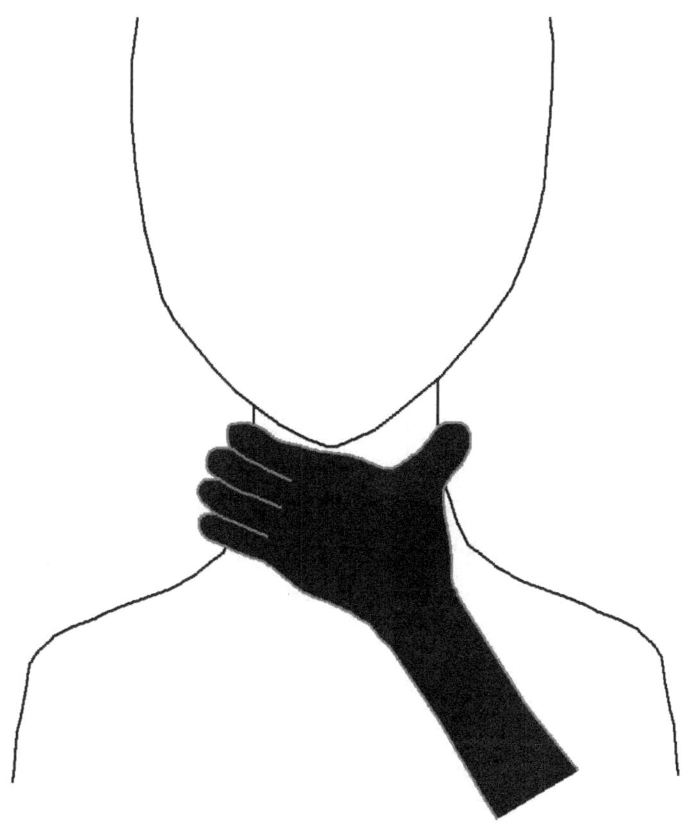

Help You

I wish I could help you

I wish I could lock up your fears
Imprison them
So they could never hurt you
So you wouldn't feel afraid

I wish I could tie up your demons
Immure them
So they would keep their distance
So you wouldn't have to run

I wish I could fix the broken pieces
Bind them
So they wouldn't break again
So you could feel unscathed

I wish I could change the world
Repair it
So it wouldn't seem so hopeless
So you could breathe in peace

And I wish I could help save you
Free you
So you wouldn't feel so trapped
So you could simply be

But I can't heal invisible wounds
and I can't fight your fears
I can't make you love yourself
or stop your flow of tears
I can't fix the world they broke
and I can't change the past
I can't reshape your memories
but we can hope they pass

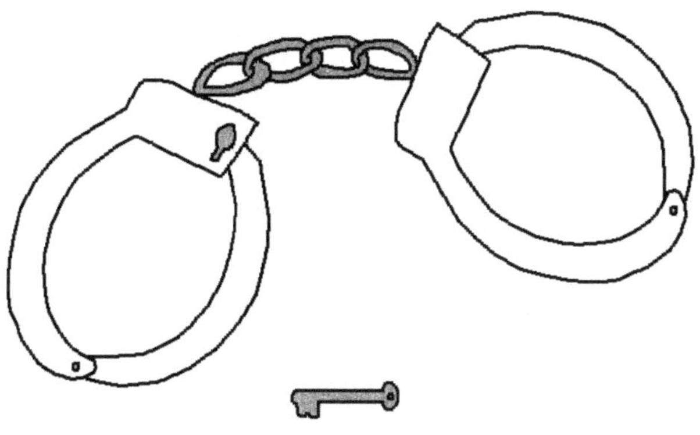

Save You

I'm sorry I couldn't save you
Wash the tears out of your eyes
Tear the sickness from your soul
Revoke your need to lie

I couldn't be what you needed then
or what you're wanting now
but I've always done my best to fight
though I never knew how

I'm sorry I couldn't fix you
Glue the cracks inside your mind
Take the pieces that don't fit
and leave them all behind

I could never make you feel proud
or prove I should belong
but I always tried to be alright
though you'd say I was wrong

I'm sorry I couldn't heal you
Find the pain and throw it out
Bring light back to what's dark again
Rid your mind of doubt

I couldn't be the hope you lost
or repair the dreams you broke
but I can still believe in you
though you're watching as I choke

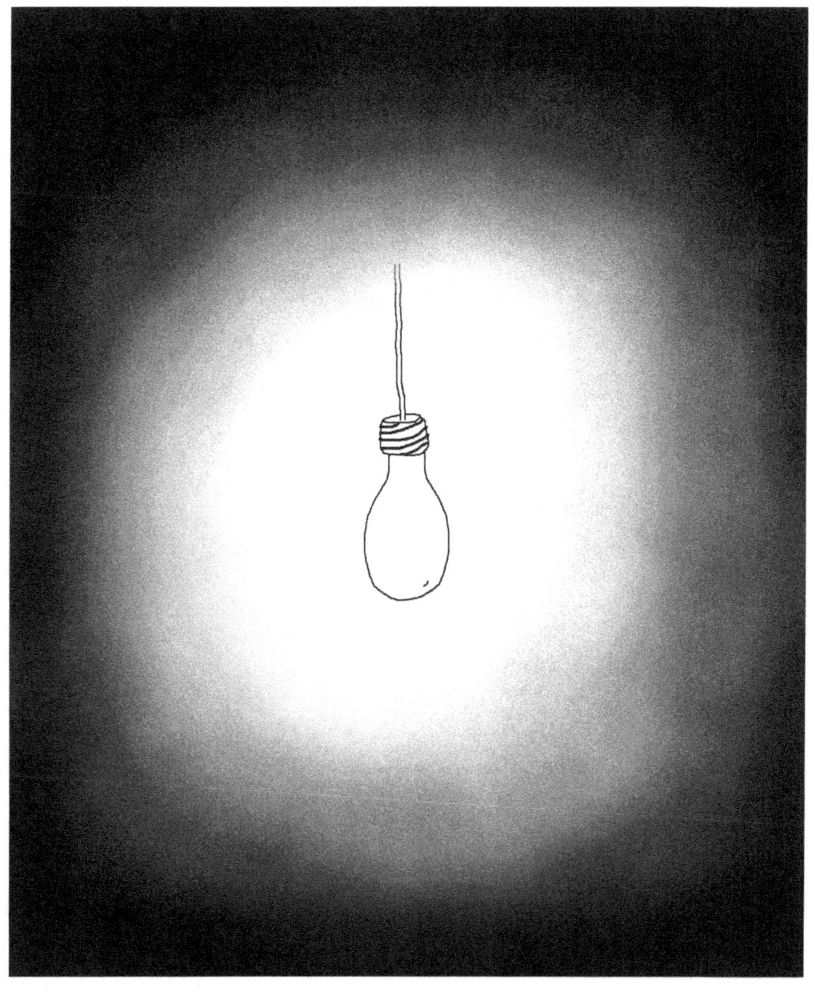

Deceit

Tell me you were made for this
Smile through tainted breath
Play the games
Stick the landing
Steal the mask from death

Tell me how you reached your dreams
Lie to save your fate
Lock the box
Bury the key
Find time to sit and wait

Tell me all your deepest fears
Shiver though it's warm
Change the rules
Hear the silence
Lose your perfect form

Tell me how the darkness crept
Sing one final song
Take a life
Fall underneath
Know the world was wrong

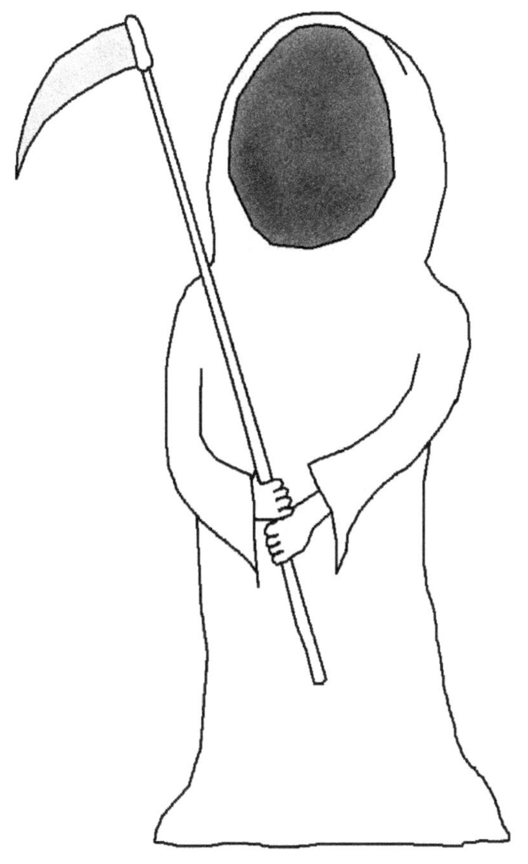

How Would You Feel?

Would you be disappointed if you knew the things I'd done?
Know my mind, see my thoughts, watch me come undone
Would you hate the time I've wasted feeling so alone?
Feel the panic, isolation, memories I've known

Would you wish we'd never met if you could read my mind?
Understand the feelings I can't seem to leave behind
Would you hate the hours we lost staring into space?
Won't it make you want to tear the skin right off your face?

Would you not want to know me if you knew the hurt I cause?
See the shadows gripping me tightly in their claws
Would you leave me in this place, frozen by my fear?
Listen to the screams that get so loud it's hard to hear

Would you lose your faith in me if you saw me cry?
Live through nightmares, skip the dreams, lose the need to try
Would you walk away if I did call out your name?
It might have been okay once, but it never will again

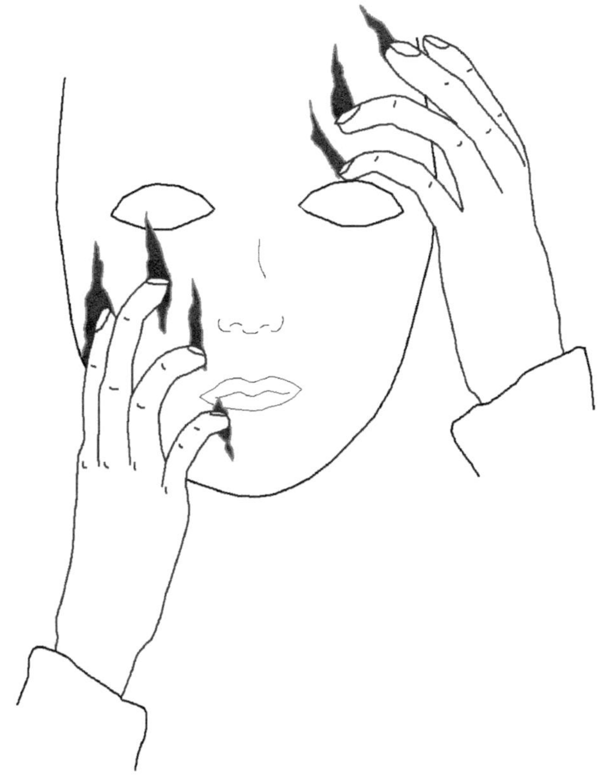

Absence

Something's missing
Lost, not found
We bury our dead things
under the ground

Something's absent
Gone far away
We lose our hope
when we forget what to say

Something's vanished
Not to be seen
We get caught up
in the things in between

Something's misplaced
Not where it should be
We fill our memories with
things others can't see

Something's astray
Not coming back
We won't be found
when we fade into black

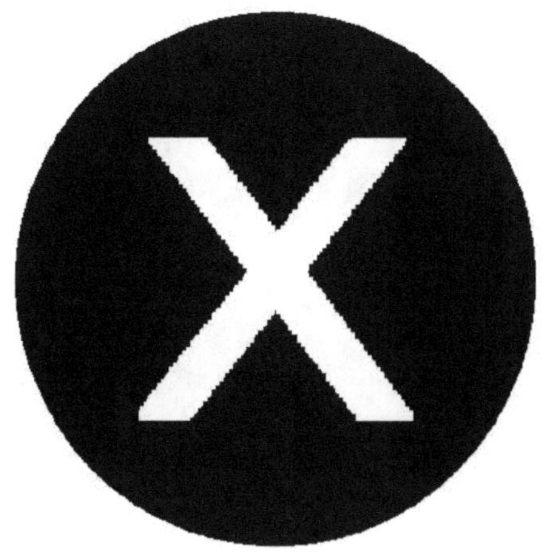

Colours

If colours could flow like the blood from our veins
From the colour of sun to the colour of rain
The brightest yellows, the coldest blues
There would be too many to ever get through
If the angriest red met the softest pink
what would orange and purple think?
The brown we touch, the grey we hide
The white of all the bones inside
If green was up instead of down
would black still make some people frown?
If colours could flow like the blood from our veins
would you see them the way they were again?

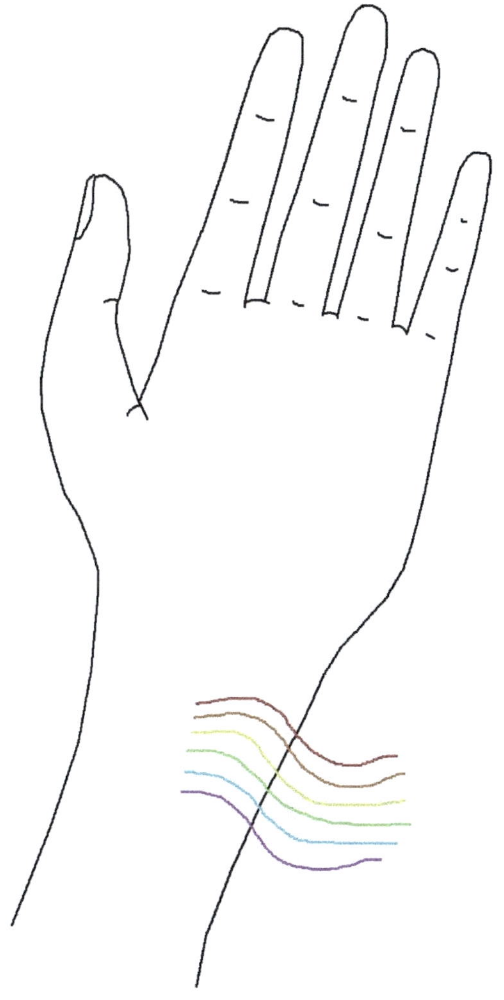

Questions

Do you feel trapped?
Do you feel alone?
Weighted down by the questions you fear
Can we make it back
to places more known?
Carry thoughts that don't age with the years

Have you known comfort?
Have you known pain?
Pierced through vitals with wounds that can't mend
What do you lose
with nothing to gain?
Fight off wars with no way to defend

Can you see reason?
Can you see trust?
Chained to the floor, waiting to drown
Will we set our minds free
of layers of dust?
Pick up pieces to put them back down

Could you live a full life?
Could you fall off young?
Crushed by all the time up until this
Would you hold regret
for the words left unsung?
Is hurt all there is we could miss?

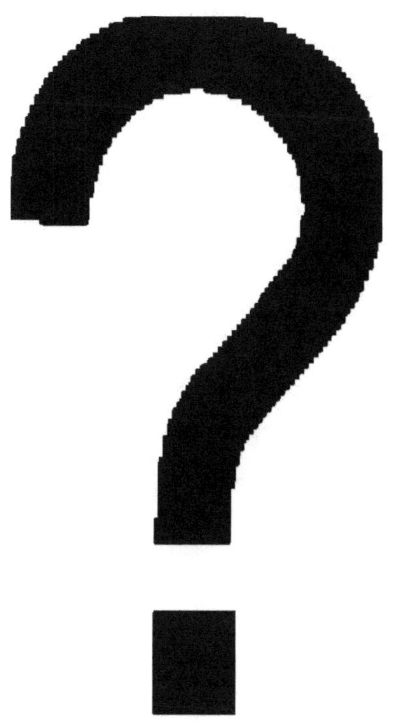

Infested

Take a deep breath, don't let go
Time still moves, too fast, too slow
I won't fall down if you hold me up
But not too tight, you might get stuck

Lost in a dream, or is this real?
We feel too much, or just don't feel
I'll still crash if we stay dormant
No peace is found with festering torment

Tied down to freedom, chained to our souls
Fuelled by obsession, a need to have goals
I'm temporary, words are eternal
Existence can be both a gift and infernal
when our fears manifest both ex and internal

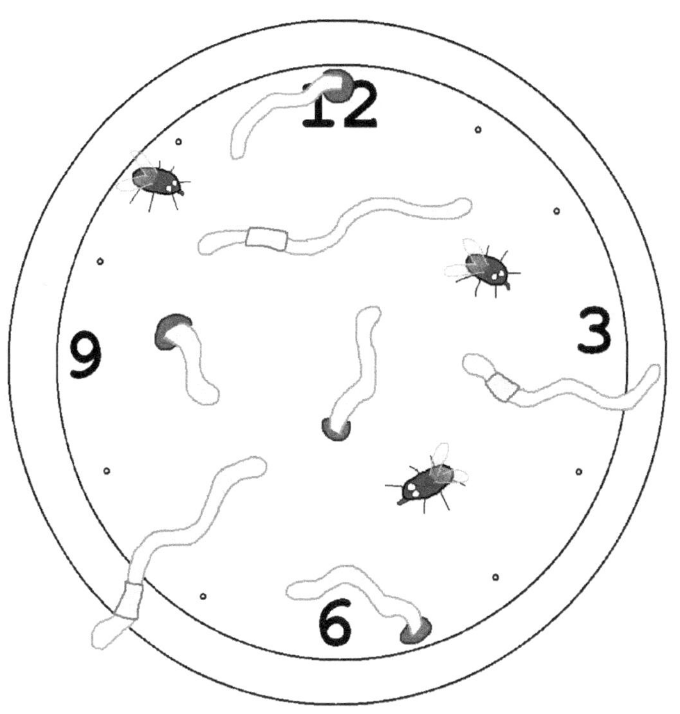

12
3
9
6

Speechless

Sit back down
You're out of line
Everything broke
and you've run out of time
to swallow your fears
Hold your head high
You start to choke
Still say it's all fine

It's over now
You got too lost
Everything hurts
and it's not worth the cost
to break through the silence
Use more than you've got
It feels like implosion
is coming in hot

But stay away
You'll never win
Everything fades
and it's hard to begin
to fight off your demons
when buried so deep
I'd give you my last breath
it's all yours to keep

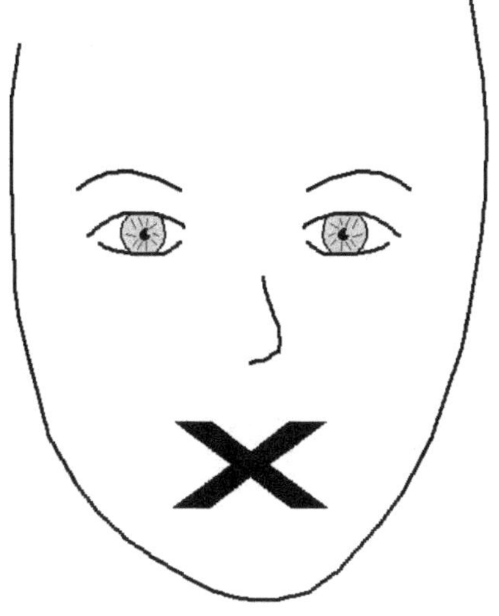

Stains

I still hear the way you screamed at me
so clearly in my head
As if it's etched upon my soul
to stay until I'm dead

I still know the way you made me feel
whenever you were mad
As if I'm still living in those moments
where every breath tastes bad

I still lock doors so I can feel safe
like I did when you were there
As if you're coming back again
to make sure I stay scared

I still see the way you looked at me
when you had had enough
As if you're still there staring
with eyes vicious and rough

I still dream about my deepest fears
of ways you would react
As if you could still get to me
Claiming your lies as fact

I still freeze up every time you speak
to brace myself for hate
As if your only capability
is inspiration to dissipate

I still flinch at every offered hug
because of how yours felt
As if they would all be the same
Like the hurt and pain yours dealt

I still have nightmares of the time
you moved your hand too fast
As if the motion could still hit
though seven years have passed

I still feel your hands upon my skin
like bugs crawling through soil
As if they'd never left their place
of discomfort and turmoil

I still hold the fear you gave to me
through many moments shared
As if time was fixed and would remain
in a place where no one cared

www.ingramcontent.com/pod-product-compliance
Lightning Source LLC
Chambersburg PA
CBHW051008050726

47592CB00007B/2762